A M E R I C A N
LIGHTHOUSES

A Pictorial History

JILL CARAVAN

COURAGE BOOKS
AN IMPRINT OF RUNNING PRESS
PHILADELPHIA · LONDON

9 8 7 6 5
Digit on the right indicates the number of this printing

Library of Congress Cataloging-in-Publication
Number 96-68393

ISBN 1-56138-788-6

This book was designed and produced by
TODTRI Book Publishers
P. O. Box 572, New York, NY 10116-0572
Fax: (212) 695-6984
e-mail: todtri @ mindspring.com

Author: Jill Caravan
Captions: Amy Handy

Publisher: Robert M. Tod
Editorial Director: Elizabeth Loonan
Book Designer: Mark Weinberg
Production Coordinator: Heather Weigel
Senior Editor: Edward Douglas
Project Editor: Cynthia Sternau
Associate Editor: Linda Greer
Picture Researcher: Laura Wyss
Desktop Associate: Michael Walther
Typesetting: Command-O, NYC

Printed and bound in Singapore

Published by Courage Books,
an imprint of
Running Press Book Publishers
125 South Twenty-second Street
Philadelphia, PA 19103-4399

PICTURE CREDITS

CONTENTS

INTRODUCTION

Lighthouses are marks and signs . . . being a matter of a high and precious nature,

in respect of salvation of ships and lives, and a kind of starlight in that element.

—FRANCIS BACON

For thousands of years, lighthouses have been welcoming beacons for all who braved the inconstancies of travel by water. The earliest travelers on the world's oceans, lakes, and rivers often needed guidance to find their way to a sheltering port, as well as to avoid dangerous rocks, sandbars, and other potentially destructive obstacles of the waterways. Bonfires, maintained on hills throughout the night, were built as beacons; thus the concept of a guiding light for sailors came into being.

Elevating the signal fires to extend the range from which they could be seen was the next logical step. The lighthouses of classical

RIGHT: The Colossus of Rhodes, built c. 292–280 B.C., was a bronze statue of the Greek sun god Helios, who held a lit torch to guide incoming ships. This spectacular work stood at the narrow entrance to the harbor for about fifty-five years before being felled by an earthquake. *Rhodes, Greece*

OPPOSITE: Yaquina Head Lighthouse exhibits elegant architectural detailing, including elaborate window ornamentation and Italianate support braces. *Newport, Oregon*

Set on a tiny island in the bay, the Pharos of Alexandria, one of the Seven Wonders of the Ancient World, was built in the third century B.C. The fires burning on the top of the tower could be seen at a distance of 100 miles. *Alexandria, Egypt*

antiquity—simple structures topped with bonfires—were built as early as the seventh century B.C. along the shores of the Mediterranean Sea.

The most famous early lighthouse in recorded history is the Pharos of Alexandria, Egypt, one of the Seven Wonders of the Ancient World. In 332 B.C., when Alexander the Great founded and laid out the city of

Alexandria, he decided to connect the nearby island of Pharos to the city by building a huge breakwater. Made of stone and masonry, it stretched almost a mile to enclose the harbor. Alexander did not live to see the completion in 290 B.C. of the remarkable 400- to 500-foot-tall, white marble lighthouse that stood at the east harbor of the island. The Pharos would have towered over the tallest existing light-

house today, which rises 348 feet at Yokohama, Japan. The light from the fires constantly maintained atop the structure was visible 100 miles out to sea. Unfortunately, the Pharos was destroyed by an earthquake in the fourteenth century.

The Colossus of Rhodes, another of the Seven Wonders of the Ancient World, also served as a beacon for ships in that busy port. The Colossus, a 120-foot bronze statue of the Greek sun god Helios, was built c. 292–280 B.C. The statue stood at the entrance to the harbor at Rhodes, bearing a lit torch in one hand to guide incoming vessels, but it guarded the seas for only about fifty-five years before being toppled by an earthquake in 224 B.C.

The Roman Empire and other Mediterranean maritime powers were leaders in the construction of the first traditional lighthouses; their systems eventually stretched from the British Islands to the Black Sea. About 100 A.D., a lighthouse known as the Tower of Hercules was built at Corunna on the northwest coast of

When Little Sable Lighthouse was constructed in 1874, the location was inaccessible by land, so all materials had to be shipped to the beach and transported to the site. *Silver Lake State Park, Michigan*

Spain, during the reign of the Emperor Trajan; repaired in 1634, it is the oldest existing building of this type in the world. During Caligula's visit to France in 40 A.D., a fire tower was built in the harbor of Boulogne; almost eight hundred years later Charlemagne returned it to service, and it became known to French sailors as the Tour d'Ordre. Other important Roman lighthouses were located in Ostia, Ravenna, and Messina, and on both sides of the English Channel; the Roman tower at Dover was later called "The Devil's Drop of Mortar" because of its durable construction.

At the beginning of the twelfth century France and Italy were the leaders in the innovation and design of new lighthouses; contemporary navigational charts note the locations of more than fifteen hundred such structures.

As technology advanced, engineering knowledge made different types of structures practical to build under often-challenging construction and weather conditions. The original Eddystone Light off the south coast of England was first illuminated in 1699. The first of four towers to be built on this dangerous rock, it was destroyed in a great storm in November 1703.

Where there was sufficiently solid rock for a strong foundation, masonry structures with a low center of gravity were erected; in other places, open-work iron or steel was used where wooden or metal piles were necessary to lay a firm foundation. (Today, some modern open-sea lighthouses resemble off-shore oil-drilling platforms, complete with helicopter landing pads and huge steel piles that extend 150 feet down into the floor of the ocean.)

FOLLOWING PAGE:
When the search for copper ore in the Great Lakes intensified in the mid-nineteenth century, the U.S. government authorized the construction of Isle Royale Lighthouse to guide vessels headed for the mines. *Menagerie Island, Michigan*

Stronger warning beacons were also developed; these were visible at far greater distances than ever before. Open bonfires were replaced by coal fires; later, tallow candles or oil lamps magnified by reflectors or focused by specially designed glass lenses were employed. Light generated from coal and acetylene gas followed, and electricity was used for the first time in 1858, at South Foreland Light in England.

In 1921, the first radio beacon for directing ships was built in New York, and from 1934 onward, radio-equipped remote-control stations began to take the place of traditional manned lighthouses.

Today, automation has rendered the tended lighthouse obsolete, for technology allows the modern beacons of civilization to function virtually without human guidance. Lamps and signal beacons are activated by radio; when daylight fades, an automatic "eye" turns on the light; and foghorns respond to an increase of moisture in the air. Yet lighthouses—symbols of human presence and safety among the uncertain elements of the natural world—continue to enchant us.

LEFT: Because it sits on a tiny island known as a nubble, Cape Neddick Lighthouse is known as Nubble Light. In addition to the keeper's dwelling, the complex also features a brick oil house and fog signal. *York, Maine*

OPPOSITE: The broad, white-washed tower of Ocracoke Light-house, one of the oldest active lights of the South-east coast, survived the Civil War intact, though the Confederates removed the lens in 1861. A new one was installed three years later. *Ocracoke, North Carolina*

CHAPTER ONE

BEACONS OF CIVILIZATION

The importance of lighthouses to Americans living along the coastlines is evident throughout our history. In fact, the Puritans, among the very first European settlers in North America, included a lighthouse in their original plans for the city that has become modern-day Boston. One of the most vital jobs in colonial days was that of the lighthouse keeper.

THE ADMINISTRATORS

During the early years in the New World, each of the thirteen colonies was responsible for the staffing and maintenance of its own aids to navigation. Congress recognized that lighthouses were a national concern, and passed an act placing their administration under national control on August 7, 1789. The new Lighthouse Service was charged with the planning, establishing, staffing, and maintaining of lighthouses, buoys, and piers along the country's coastal waters. All American lighthouses and lightships were under this administration until the establishment in 1852 of a new administrative body, the nine-member Lighthouse Board.

"The lighthouse and lightship appeal to the interest and better instinct of man because they are symbolic of never-ceasing watchfulness, of steadfast endurance in every exposure, of widespread helpfulness. The building and the keeping of the lights is a picturesque and humanitarian work of

RIGHT: **The tower now standing on Bodie Island, lighted in 1872, is the third on the site. The first tilted irreparably out of alignment; the second fell victim to Confederate explosives.** *Cape Hatteras National Seashore, Oregon Inlet, North Carolina*

OPPOSITE: **Constructed in 1858 on Mount Desert Island to guide vessels into the harbor, Bass Harbor Head Lighthouse draws many visitors with its warm glow and romantic setting.** *Acadia National Park, Maine*

An elegant essay in stone, these stairs of Concord Point Lighthouse were once traveled by a veteran of the War of 1812, who served as the tower's first keeper when it was built in 1827. *Havre de Grace, Maryland*

equipment than any other country. Significant advances, including the introduction of radio beacons and electric buoys, and technical improvements such as fog signals were also made.

In 1939 the Lighthouse Bureau was abolished by the Presidential Reorganization Act of 1939. All its activities and personnel were placed under the authority of the U.S. Coast Guard, where it remains to this day.

THE KEEPERS

Most lighthouses today are equipped with automatic lights that require very little tending. A regular, but widely spread, series of service calls is all that is required to maintain these most useful structures—a far cry from the twenty-four-hour attention that was necessary for the maintenance of the early lights.

Before automation, the old-fashioned lighthouse keepers—the men and women who lived in or near the lighthouses they tended, and whose sworn duty it was to keep the lights burning—had jobs entailing enormous responsibility for the safety of others' lives. However, the lives of the

the nation." So wrote George R. Putnam, first commissioner of the U.S. Bureau of Lighthouses. Putnam's appointment followed a massive reorganization of the Lighthouse Board implemented by an act of Congress, which established the Bureau of Lighthouses in 1910. By 1924, under Putnam's tenure, the U.S. Lighthouse Service was the largest in the world, with more automatic

LEFT: **Like many coastal lights south of New England, Cape May Lighthouse is set on low ground, necessitating a tall tower. The first Cape May tower fell victim to erosion soon after it was built in 1823.** *Cape May, New Jersey*

OPPOSITE: **Set at New Jersey's southernmost point, Cape May Lighthouse guides shipping in Delaware Bay. Its 600,000-candlepower light soars 165 feet above sea level.** *Cape May, New Jersey*

Though it made construction arduous, the rocky perch of Yaquina Head Lighthouse provides a gloriously picturesque setting. *Newport, Oregon*

RIGHT: Lost to erosion in 1984, Great Point Light was reconstructed to duplicate the appearance of its original 1818 tower. *National Wildlife Refuge, Nantucket Island, Massachusetts*

OPPOSITE: Barcelona Lighthouse, erected on Lake Erie in 1829, was one of the first lighthouses on the Great Lakes. The ancient appearance of its fieldstone tower attests to the fact that its use was discontinued in 1859. *Barcelona, New York*

lighthouse keepers themselves were isolated, lonely, and filled with tedious repetition. Every day at dusk the several lamps of the towers had to be lit, and sometime around midnight every night the lamps needed to have their fuel replenished; every morning the lamps had to be extinguished, and every day during daylight hours the lamps required cleaning and polishing to maintain their optimum brightness.

The lighthouse keeper's job entailed almost constant labor. The title of keeper, or first or second assistant keeper, implied much more than the mere tending of the light in the tower. The safety mechanisms associated with the central purpose of the facility—the light, the foghorn, and the radio—topped the maintenance and repair list at all times,

but keepers at all levels were also expected to maintain the lighthouse, accompanying buildings, and grounds in top condition. Lighthouse inspectors were vigilant in their scheduled visits; not surprisingly, an underground network of keepers flourished, alerting one another to the impending appearance of the inspectors.

Men did not have exclusive rights to this difficult job. During the Revolutionary War, Hannah Thomas kept the lights of Gurnet Point Lighthouse in Plymouth, Massachusetts, burning while her husband was busy defending America; she may have been the first woman in the federal service. Hundreds more women have tended American lighthouses over the years, many of them as official keepers.

Only twenty-six feet high, Owl's Head Lighthouse is set on a high promontory, bringing its light to a focal plane of one hundred feet and making it visible sixteen miles at sea. *Rockland, Maine*

OPPOSITE: The strikingly painted Otter Island Lighthouse keeps watch on Lake Superior's northern shore. *Ontario*

The conical 65-foot tower of Umpqua River Lighthouse is part of a large complex completed in 1894 that included two dwellings and two oil houses. *Winchester Bay, Oregon*

Umpqua River Lighthouse boasts the only red lens on the West Coast, with a focal plane 165 feet above sea level. Viewed from inside, the effect is almost kaleidoscopic. *Winchester Bay, Oregon*

RIGHT: Looking like a typical New England farmhouse, the clapboard dwelling of Pemaquid Point Lighthouse was built in 1857, thirty years after the tower. The building is now home to the Fisherman's Museum. *John's Bay, Maine*

OPPOSITE: The very first lighthouse in the Ocracoke area was built in 1798 near the spot once inhabited by the notorious pirate Blackbeard. A second tower, from 1803, was destroyed by lightning in 1818. The existing tower has stood since 1823, making it one of the oldest active lights of the Southeast coast. *Ocracoke, North Carolina*

The bronze door of Cape Hatteras Lighthouse, set in an imposing surround ornamented with Italian marble, refutes the traditional concept of the lighthouse as a severely functional structure. *Buxton, Dare County, North Carolina*

Set on the eastern shore of Delaware Bay near Cape May, the red-roofed East Point Lighthouse emits a red beam to aid shipping in the bay. *East Point, New Jersey*

EARLY LIGHTS

The Puritans, who settled Boston in 1630, erected one of the first lighthouses in America on their peninsular home of Trimountaine (named for the site's three hills). One of these, Beacon Hill, was even named for this purpose. Boston Light, the earliest lighthouse in the United States, was built in 1716; destroyed by the British during the American Revolution, it was rebuilt in 1783.

According to newspaper accounts, Boston Light stood for 201 years before it flew the American flag. According to the *Boston Globe* on June 27, 1917, there was never any money in the lighthouse's budget to buy a flag, and so none was flown. This oversight was corrected with much pomp and circumstance that same year. Charles F. Weed, the president of the Boston Chamber of Commerce, gathered fifty dollars in donations to buy the first flag from a group of visiting dignitaries who had taken a tour of the lighthouse. Since then, the American flag has flown there, usually one that was previously displayed over the White House.

FOLLOWING PAGE:
The 108-foot tower of Montauk Point Lighthouse was designed by architect John McComb, Jr., and built in 1797 of "Chatham freestone, fine hammered." Concerted efforts to protect the station from serious erosion have met with some success. *Long Island, New York*

LEFT: Price Creek Lighthouse once guided shipping at the mouth of the Cape Fear River, part of a treacherous expanse of waters along the southern coast of North Carolina. *Southport, North Carolina*

The first twenty-three lighthouses built in colonies of the United States were constructed prior to the nineteenth century. The first lighthouse built under the auspices of the Lighthouse Service was erected at the easternmost point on Long Island, New York, in 1797 by order of President George Washington. It stands proudly today on the steep cliff of Montauk Point.

The Owls Head Lighthouse, built at the south end of the inlet to Penobscot Bay, Maine, was once a refuge for pirates who plundered the rich shipping lanes in the Isles of Shoals off the coast. Later, writers such as Nathaniel Hawthorne, James Whittier, and Harriet Beecher Stowe frequented the same islands, possibly drawing inspiration from the light of the distant beacon.

The Portland Headlight in Maine, a towering construction of cast-iron, is another lighthouse that was built under orders from George Washington. It is often claimed to be the most photographed lighthouse in the United States. As is the custom in many historic lighthouses, the keeper's quarters now house a small museum.

ABOVE: Stationed on the site of the country's oldest lighthouse, the current Boston Light was built in 1783, to replace the tower of 1716 that was blown up during the Revolution. *Boston Harbor, Massachusetts*

OPPOSITE: Put into service in 1791, Portland Head Light was only partially completed when local control of lighthouses was turned over to the federal government. It was the first tower to be finished by the new government. *Portland, Maine*

CHAPTER TWO

HOME OF
THE LIGHT

Seafaring navigators find their way across the oceans by four principle means of navigation: piloting, electronic navigation, dead reckoning, and celestial navigation. Lighthouses play an important role in two of these techniques—piloting and electronic navigation.

NAVIGATION

The art and science of piloting involves the guiding of a ship from its departure point to its destination. The pilot follows landmarks, both natural and man-made, and takes soundings to determine the water's depth in order to avoid underwater hazards. Lighthouses and their kin—lightships and light buoys—are of primary importance among the easily distinguishable man-made landmarks.

With their strategic siting and pre-existing use in marine navigation, lighthouses were a natural choice for the location of many of the radio transmitting stations employed in modern electronic navigation. The electronic equipment on the ship receives the radio waves, whose direction and duration are converted into navigational data. The navigator then uses this information to get a fix on the present location and chart a course to the ship's destination.

Lighthouses have no more than coincidental roles in dead reckoning and celestial navigation. When using dead reckoning (or deduced reckoning), the navigator plots the ship's whereabouts by maintaining very careful records of how far the vessel has traveled from the known point of

RIGHT: **Portland Head Light still retains its picture-postcard charm and lovely nineteenth-century keeper's quarters, despite undergoing automation in 1989 during ceremonies marking the bicentennial of the U.S. lighthouse system.** *Portland, Maine*

OPPOSITE: **The warm yellow glow of Portland Head Light—produced by a second-order Fresnel lens—shines amid a symphony of bluish gray surroundings.** *Portland, Maine*

RIGHT: **Boston Harbor Lighthouse utilizes a second-order Fresnel lens. The 21-inch reflectors on the lantern's lamps earned the station a reputation for the best reflector lights in the United States.** *Little Brewster Island, Massachusetts*

departure. The sun, moon, and stars provide the "map" for navigators employing the old-fashioned celestial method. The navigator calculates the ship's position by using a sextant to determine the altitude of the celestial bodies above the horizon and a chronometer to determine longitude.

ILLUMINATION

As technology improved, lighthouse illumination became easier and more cost efficient. Wood was the fuel for the first signal fires, followed by coal and then oil. Each advance in technology provided lighthouse keepers with longer-burning, more reliable sources for their warning lights.

LEFT: **An aerial view of the Cape Hatteras National Seashore discloses the spectacular setting of Cape Hatteras Lighthouse, the state symbol of North Carolina.** *Buxton, Dare County, North Carolina*

OPPOSITE: **Topped with a scarlet lantern housing a first-order lens, St. Augustine Lighthouse sports a lively swirl of black and white that serves to make it more visible by day.** *Anastasia Island, Florida*

The electric filament lamp became the standard in the 1920s. This technology has held the predominant role in lighthouse illumination ever since. Joseph Swan, an English physicist, first developed the filament light in 1860. Both Swan and Thomas Edison—after the necessary vacuum technologies had advanced considerably—independently produced serviceable light bulbs. These early bulbs had carbon filaments that burned away quickly, though they produced a white light rather than the less desirable yellow light.

Kerosene, in vapor form, was a commonly used fuel for a few years in the very early 1900s, but that trend quickly faded. Thanks to the pioneering work of Sweden's Gustaf Dalen, the fuel of choice soon became acetylene gas. Dalen's new technology came into widespread use around 1910, allowing extremely remote, automated lighthouses to be constructed. The acetylene-powered systems could be set up and maintained by an annual visit to renew the gas supply and check on the system. He also invented the Dalen light, which kindles automatically at dusk and extinguishes automatically at dawn, for use in unmanned lighthouses.

Since the area around Point Bonita Lighthouse is so often blanketed by fog, the lantern and second-order lens of the original 1855 tower—which had soared 306 feet over the sea—were moved nearby to a new tower in 1877. At 140 feet above sea level, this light is more easily seen below the fog line.

RIGHT: Invented in 1822, the Fresnel lens revolutionized lighthouse illumination. This first-order lens is displayed at Cape Hatteras Lighthouse, in the double keeper's dwelling that now serves a museum devoted to the history of the lighthouse. *Buxton, Dare County, North Carolina*

OPPOSITE: Installed in Rock of Ages Lighthouse in 1910, this second-order flashing Fresnel lens served faithfully for three-quarters of a century. It is now displayed at the Windigo Ranger Station in Isle Royale National Park. *Isle Royale, Michigan*

LIGHT AND SOUND

Numerous methods have been employed since the early eighteenth century to increase the intensity and range of beacon lights. The Fresnel lens, a central disk surrounded by a series of concentric rings, invented in 1822, was the predecessor of today's light-projection technology.

French physicist Augustin Jean Fresnel was the first man to show that two beams of light will not interfere with each other if they are polarized in different planes. That discovery led him to deduce that light and sound travel in a transverse wave motion, rather than longitudinally. He developed a number of basic formulas for reflection, refraction, and polarization, as well as the famous Fresnel lens, which produces the parallel beams of light used in lighthouses and some theatrical spotlights. Fresnel designed seven orders of lens, from the giant first-order lens employed as a seacoast light to the small sixth-order lens used as a harbor light.

ABOVE: The fifth-order lens of Yaquina Bay Lighthouse ushered vessels into the bay for just three years (1871 to 1874) when the Lighthouse Board deemed it unnecessary in favor of the nearby Yaquina Head light. *Newport, Oregon*

OPPOSITE: Housing the original fourth-order lens of the 1871 Trinidad Head Lighthouse, a replica of the lighthouse, erected by local citizens, stands beside the original fog bell. The compact structure, intended to guide vessels traveling close to shore, was placed on a hillside that raised its light to 196 feet above the sea. *Trinidad, California*

The pedestal of Grosse Point Lighthouse on Lake Michigan supports a second-order Fresnel lens. The device behind the pedestal houses the clockwork mechanism that rotates the lens. *Evanston, Illinois*

LEFT: The keeper's existence was made arduous by many factors, not least of which may have been the incessant journey up and down a steep, narrow staircase. At a height of 46 feet, Beaver Island Lighthouse required a shorter climb than many; nevertheless the stairs must at times have seemed to spiral endlessly. *Beaver Island, Michigan*

BELOW: The bold spiral painted around the outside of Cape Hatteras Lighthouse is echoed in the decoration of the inside. Looking down through the center of the staircase, the tower's interior takes on the appearance of an abstract graphic design. *Buxton, Dare County, North Carolina*

Varying combinations of mirrors, lenses, and prisms are now used to optimize the efficiency of lighthouse beacons, some of which can be seen from nearly thirty miles away, although the average range is about twenty miles. Incandescent lamps are the usual choice for a light source in modern lighthouses. The light from these lamps is concentrated and projected through a series of lenses similar to those found at airports. Lighthouse lanterns have also been designed to rotate at regular, pre-set rates to allow the beacon to be seen from all directions.

Electricity provides the power for modern lighthouses and their lights, which can range up to twenty-eight million candlepower in intensity. The more powerful beacons are generally found in areas with heavier traffic, more severe weather conditions, and adverse visibility.

Identifying the warning beacon of a lighthouse is as important to navigators as simply seeing the lighthouse. To this end, each lighthouse is assigned its own character of light, or code. These characteristics can include variations in the intensity and/or color of the light, the flashing frequency, and the light's elevation.

To combat the dangerous effects of bad weather, such as fog, on beacon lights, modern lighthouses also have a wide array of sound-emitting devices incorporated into their systems; like the lights, these serve to guide and warn off ships. Bells and explosives were among the first of these devices available, but today the familiar foghorn is the industry standard. The most powerful of these, the diaphone, employs compressed air to produce a sound with a range of as far as eight miles. And, of course, when developing technology produced weather-defeating innovations such as radio waves and radar beacons (called racons), those too became a part of the operative lighthouse technology.

FOLLOWING PAGE: Situated on the eastern shore of Lake Michigan, this lighthouse endures the ferocious impact of turbulent waves during a violent storm. *Frankfort, Michigan*

RIGHT: Set high on the bluffs of the central Oregon coast, the 93-foot Yaquina Head Lighthouse, lighted in 1873, shines its beam 163 feet above the sea. *Newport, Oregon*

OPPOSITE: Reflecting by nomenclature the culture of the settlers' origin, New London Harbor Lighthouse sits on the Thames River. The 88-foot octagonal tower still operates; erected in 1801, it is the oldest lighthouse in Connecticut. *New London, Connecticut*

LIGHTSHIPS AND BUOYS

In the seventeenth century, a supplement to the lighthouse began to surface on the oceans and waterways in those spots where lighthouses were not a practical solution. Lightships may not have the permanence of their land-based forbears; nevertheless, they are equipped with the same equipment found in lighthouses.

In safer waters, unmanned lightships and buoys provide the necessary directional guidance. Even in some open-sea locations, very large, lighted buoys, towering as high as fourteen feet over the water, have come into play as new technologies have made them feasible.

The waters also contain signaling devices that are not readily apparent to the casual observer. Oscillators and bells are an example of this hidden technology; these produce underwater signals—at hazardous locations such as reefs and the entrances to harbors—that are picked up by shipboard instruments and used to safely guide the ship along its way.

Aglow in the ghostly fog, the first-order Fresnel lens of Heceta Head Lighthouse emits a bright beacon from the tower's perch on the jagged rocks near Devil's Elbow State Park. *Florence, Oregon*

In areas where fixed light towers were problematic—such as the perilous Nantucket Shoals—lightships could provide a more practical solution. Officially known as LV-112, Lightship Nantucket served from 1936 to 1975, when it was decommissioned. It now visits various Atlantic ports for public viewing and spends winters in Portland, Maine. It was succeeded by the still-active WLV-612.

On the western shore of Lake Michigan, the bright red tower of Kenosha Pierhead Light stands in opposition to the white of winter. *Kenosha, Wisconsin*

Rising from the sand dunes, Ponce de Leon Inlet Lighthouse projects its beam nineteen miles. The area was originally called Mosquito Inlet because the insects flourished in the humid swamps nearby, hindering construction of the lighthouse. *Ponce de Leon Inlet, Florida*

RIGHT: The spectral form of the ice-draped St. Joseph North Pierhead Light appears almost supernatural. Captured during a lull in a Lake Michigan blizzard, the image dramatically evokes the loneliness and isolation that often characterized the keeper's life. *St. Joseph River, Michigan*

OPPOSITE: The candy cane colors of West Quoddy Head Lighthouse are topped by a black lantern housing a third-order lens, 83 feet above sea level. The banding, designed to make the tower more visible to ships in daylight, has also made this one of the better-known lighthouses. *Lubec, Maine*

MODERN LIGHTHOUSE ADMINISTRATION

Given their critical nature for trade and transportation, lighthouses in most countries are generally under the control of the national government. In the United States, the agency of responsibility is the U.S. Coast Guard; in Canada, it is the Aids of Navigation Division of the Department of Transportation. The Coast Guard is responsible for overseeing about 167 manned lighthouses, twelve thousand unmanned lights, twenty-six thousand buoys (lighted and unlighted), and several thousand other navigational aides, including many fog signals.

LEFT: A window in Bald Head Lighthouse affords some daylight to the stairs of the octagonal tower, which was built in 1818 and is no longer active. *Smith Island, North Carolina*

OPPOSITE: The stylish Yaquina Head Lighthouse—the second oldest active light on the state's coast—still uses its original first-order lens. *Newport, Oregon*

CHAPTER THREE

LIGHTHOUSES:
PAST AND PRESENT

THE NORTHEAST

Throughout the Colonial period and well into the nineteenth century, the great majority of American lighthouses were concentrated in New England, where the shipping industry of the era was based. Thirty of the forty lighthouses constructed between the end of the Revolution and 1820 were located north of Delaware Bay, indicative of the region's heavy maritime traffic, as well as its rocky, island-strewn, and often fog-bound coast.

With its great stretch of craggy shore and its myriad islands, Maine requires a tremendous number of lighthouses. When George Washington ordered the construction of Portland

Headlight in 1791, Maine was still part of the Massachusetts colony. Presiding over the entrance to Portland Harbor, the light has been in continuous use since its construction and remains virtually unchanged except for some minor alterations and equipment upgrades. The quintessential New England look of the keeper's quarters dates from the nineteenth century, and the former oil house adjoining the tower now houses a small museum of lighthouse memorabilia.

The dangers of navigating the New England coast are often intensified by fog, so in 1820 the West Quoddy Head Lighthouse in Lubec, Maine, became the first in the nation to use a fog bell. The very first fog signal in the U. S. colonies

RIGHT: **The lovely but perilous setting of the Pemaquid Point Light was the scene of one of the worst shipwrecks in Maine history, when the schooner** *George F. Edmunds* **ran off course in 1903.** *John's Bay, Maine*

OPPOSITE: **Perched on the rocky coast of Mount Desert Island, the Bass Harbor Head Lighthouse was built in 1858 to help vessels maneuver into the harbor.** *Acadia National Park, Maine*

The plain Grindel Point Lighthouse, decommissioned in 1934, was preserved through the efforts of local citizens as a memorial to the seafarers of the island.
Isleboro Island, Maine

was a fog cannon, installed at the country's first lighthouse, Boston Light, in 1719. Brant Point was the site of the country's second lighthouse, built in 1746 at the entrance to Nantucket Harbor.

Nantucket is also the site of Great Point Light, the first of only two light stations controlled by a state government after the country declared independence. This occurred before the United States government assumed responsibility for navigational aids in 1789. In the early nineteenth century, the world's most heavily trafficked waters outside England were those of the New England sounds; hence the Massachusetts coast features numerous lighthouses. Martha's Vineyard, just to the northwest of Nantucket Island, possesses five lights; another early Massachusetts light was built at Gurnet Point on Plymouth Bay in 1769 and turned over to the federal government in 1790.

The Stonington light station, with its castlelike turret and keeper's quarters, was moved in 1840 from its original location in Stonington Harbor to protect the building from erosion. The local historical society now maintains it as a historic house.
Stonington, Connecticut

Drum Point Lighthouse, an interesting screwpile structure built in 1883 at the entrance to the Patuxent River, was moved two miles upriver to the Calvert Marine Museum in 1975. Restored to prime condition, the lighthouse is now open to the public. *Calvert County, Maryland*

The great need for a lighthouse at the east entrance to Block Island Sound was clearly demonstrated when the lighthouse itself was destroyed in 1815 in one of the sudden storms common to the area. The sturdy tower now on the spot was built in 1857. *Point Judith, Rhode Island*

Gurnet Point featured the first twin light towers in the Colonies. From a short distance, however, they appeared to be a single light, so one eventually fell into disuse; the one that remains is known as Plymouth Lighthouse. *Plymouth Bay, Massachusetts*

One of the most crucial lights of Rhode Island stands at the Point Judith Harbor of Refuge, where the waters of Narragansett Bay and Long Island Sound rush together. The original 1810 tower, destroyed in the gale of 1816, was replaced by a stone tower; the current octagonal granite tower was later painted brown on the upper half and white on the lower to make it more visible by day.

The state of Connecticut turned over its lighthouses to the federal government in 1790, thirty years after erecting the Colonies' fourth lighthouse, at New London Harbor. The station served as a testing site for fog signal equipment in the mid-nineteenth century. The quaint charm of the Stonington Harbor Lighthouse—

decommissioned in 1889 in favor of the Stonington Breakwater Light—has been preserved by the Stonington Historical Society as a maritime museum.

The most famous of New York's lighthouses is the Montauk Point Light, guarding the southern entrance to Long Island Sound. Built in 1797 by John McComb, one of the country's earliest well-known architects, the Montauk tower was set upon a bluff that brought the light to 160 feet above sea level. This lighthouse, declared "a very important light" by the Lighthouse Board in the nineteenth century, is today threatened by drastic erosion, though efforts to control it have slowed the deterioration of the site.

Perhaps the first lighthouse completed by the new government after the Revolution was Portland Head Light. Because the fledgling government had so little money, George Washington advised the builders to use materials found in the immediate vicinity. *Portland, Maine*

At least five structures were successively built and destroyed at Brant Point, though the first one, built in 1746, managed to survive the Revolution. The current Brant Point Lighthouse, erected in 1900, is the lowest light in New England. *Nantucket Island, Massachusetts*

LEFT: The strikingly banded West Quoddy Head Lighthouse—situated at the easternmost point of the continental United States—guides vessels around Campobello Island and through the dangerous waters of the Bay of Fundy. *Lubec, Maine*

OPPOSITE: Many shipwrecks occurred near the Great Point Light in the latter nineteenth century, when vessels confused the lighthouse with the nearby Cross Rip lightship. *National Wildlife Refuge, Nantucket Island, Massachusetts*

THE SOUTHEAST

The ocean has taken more than two thousand ships since the time of Colonial America; everything from wooden sailing craft to German U-boats litters the ocean floor. Yet even the presence of numerous lighthouses did not prevent the dangerous stretch of coastline along the Outer Banks of North Carolina from being dubbed the "Graveyard of the Atlantic." Cape Hatteras Lighthouse, one of several standing guard over the region, was considered the most important East Coast light in the nineteenth century. It is still the tallest lighthouse in the country, underscoring the fact that the lower coastline of the South requires higher towers to make the light visible far out at sea, compared to the North, where lighthouses could be built atop the elevated rocky shore.

The distinctive patterning of the Cape Hatteras tower is typical of many lighthouses. In order to be more easily seen by sailors during the day, towers were often painted in two contrasting colors. Black and white was the combination generally favored along southern shores, as evidenced also by the lighthouses at Cape Lookout and Bodie Island in North Carolina, Cape Henry in Virginia Beach, and Cape Canaveral and St.

LEFT: **Captured on a gloriously bright day, the pristine Key West Lighthouse pays tribute to the dedicated preservationists who restored the dilapidated tower and reopened it in 1989.** *Key West, Florida*

RIGHT: **The purplish cast of a stormy sky provides a sharp contrast to the black-and-white Cape Lookout Lighthouse. The diamond pattern, added in 1873 to make the tower a more visible day mark, prompted a nearby community to call itself Diamond City.** *Cape Lookout National Seashore, North Carolina*

RIGHT: Rumored to be haunted, St. Simons Island Lighthouse was rebuilt in the 1870s after the Confederates destroyed the original tower during the Civil War. With sickness plaguing the work crew, construction took nearly three years. *Brunswick Harbor, Georgia*

BELOW: The red-framed windows of the soaring Cape Hatteras Light stand out against its graceful spiral pattern. *Buxton, Dare County, North Carolina*

LEFT: Nicknamed "Old Baldy," the Bald Head Lighthouse exhibits an air of elegant deterioration. Deactivated in 1935, it is now open to the public as a museum. *Smith Island, North Carolina*

OPPOSITE: The oldest of the state's many lighthouses, the soaring octagonal tower at Bald Head was built to guide ships around the alarmingly named Cape Fear. *Smith Island, North Carolina*

Augustine in Florida. Among North Carolina's other important lights is that at Currituck Beach. Built in 1874 to illuminate the one remaining dark stretch of the south Atlantic coast, this lighthouse was deemed essential in helping southbound vessels that sailed close to shore to avoid the dangers of the north-flowing Gulf Stream.

One of Georgia's lighthouses has found its way into the vernacular of the state's residents in the expression "from Raburn Gap to Tybee Light," referring to the fact that the elevation of the state falls from nearly a mile above sea level right down to the ocean. The highest point in the state, Brasstown Bald Mountain near Raburn Gap in northeastern Georgia, climbs to 4,784 feet above sea level; Tybee Island Lighthouse, erected in 1742 (one of the first publicly built structures in Georgia), stands at sea level at the entrance to the port of Savannah.

Construction of southern lighthouses, particularly in Florida, could be difficult and dangerous for workers due to sweltering heat and swarms of insects that brought the constant threat of disease, especially malaria. Many a work crew succumbed to illness under these conditions.

Also a hindrance to construction were the soft, sandy coasts of the South, since they often proved too insubstantial to anchor a structure. Hence the pile lighthouse was developed in the mid-nineteenth century, whereby piles driven deep into the seabed provided a firmer foundation. The Chesapeake Bay area features a number of screw-pile lights, including the Thomas Point Shoal Lighthouse, and the Drum Point Lighthouse, originally situated on the Patuxent River.

Seemingly dwarfed by surrounding trees, the 64-foot Amelia Island Lighthouse projects its beacon 107 feet above the sea. *Fernandina Beach, Florida*

RIGHT: **Fort Jefferson, begun in 1846, was constructed around an existing lighthouse; in 1876 a new light was built atop a staircase within the fort. Though long inactive, this lighthouse is in good condition, and the fort itself is now a national monument.** *Dry Tortugas, Florida*

OPPOSITE: **The distinctive black-and-white bands of the Bodie Island Lighthouse were painted on the rebuilt lighthouse in the 1870s to improve its visibility by day.** *Cape Hatteras National Seashore, Oregon Inlet, North Carolina*

Perhaps the most picturesque lighthouse on the Great Lakes, Split Rock on Lake Superior also features a separate fog signal building capped by large foghorns. *Castle Danger, Minnesota*

THE GREAT LAKES

The lighthouses of the Great Lakes were honored with a series of postage stamps—featuring the work of artist Howard Koslow—first issued by the U.S. Postal Service on June 17, 1995. The official first-day issue was held on board the Coast Guard icebreaker *Mackinaw* on Lake Huron at Cheboygan, Michigan, practically in the shadow of River Range Front Lighthouse.

Marblehead Light, located between Cleveland and Toledo, Ohio, is the oldest continuously operating lighthouse on the Great Lakes. It was built in 1818 as a beacon for Lake Erie's travelers in an area particularly prone to severe storms. Lake Michigan's St. Joseph Light, built in 1832 in St. Joseph, Michigan, features a unique twin-tower design with an elevated walkway spanning the distance between the towers.

A dangerously hidden reef that lurked just beneath the waters of Lake Huron spurred the construction of Spectacle Reef Light in 1870. Thirty-Mile Point Lighthouse was also erected to warn off boats from hidden shoals and sandbars; these are located at the mouth of New York's Niagara River where it empties into Lake Ontario.

Split Rock Lighthouse, dramatically sited on a cliff nearly 170 feet above Lake Superior (near Duluth, Minnesota), was built in 1910 as a reaction to a disastrous and deadly winter storm. Five years earlier, the unanticipated blizzard had sunk thirty ore boats and freighters and killed dozens of crewmen.

Big Sable Point Lighthouse, still an important station on Lake Michigan, was built in 1867 after the Lighthouse Board realized the need for a light at the last remaining dark spot on the eastern shore of the lake. To provide a better daymark, the tower was painted black across the middle third, with the upper and lower thirds white. As exemplified by the Grand Haven South Pierhead Inner Light, the lights south of Big Sable are all pierhead lights, since ships bound south for larger ports head to shipping lanes farther into the lake after passing Big Sable.

ABOVE: **Encased in steel plates painted a vivid red, the dwelling of Holland Harbor South Pierhead Lighthouse sports a gabled roof that testifies to the Dutch influence prevalent in the region.** *Holland Harbor, Michigan*

OPPOSITE: **Now the centerpiece of a state park, Split Rock Lighthouse rises 130 feet above Lake Superior. The spectacular setting made construction difficult, entailing the use of a derrick to raise over 300 tons of material to the site.** *Castle Danger, Minnesota*

Gothic in style and built of local brownstone, Sand Island Lighthouse features an octagonal tower rising from the corner of the keeper's dwelling. *Apostle Islands, Wisconsin*

RIGHT: Devils Island Lighthouse once sported fluted braces at the base, but today a steel exoskeleton lends additional support to the slim cylinder. Its site on Lake Superior is bordered by sea caves. *Apostle Islands, Wisconsin*

OPPOSITE: The 107-foot tower of Little Sable Lighthouse was originally whitewashed to distinguish it from the black-and-white Big Sable, but the paint has now disappeared, exposing rich red brick. *Silver Lake State Park, Michigan*

ABOVE: **Guarding a rocky stretch of the Pacific, Point Arena Lighthouse was devastated by the earthquake of 1906; it was rebuilt of reinforced concrete two years later.** *Point Arena, California*

THE WEST COAST

When California and the Oregon Territory became part of the United States in the mid-nineteenth century, there had never been a lighthouse along the whole long stretch of coast. The first light on the West Coast was situated on Alcatraz Island in 1852, but was torn down in 1909 to clear space for the prison. The Point Pinos Lighthouse at Monterey, California—the third lighthouse to be built on the West Coast—is now the oldest working light on that coast. It managed to withstand (with some damage) the earthquake that destroyed San Francisco in 1906, but the Point Arena Lighthouse, south of Mendocino, was not so fortunate, losing its tower, lens, and dwelling to the earthquake.

The California coast is particularly susceptible to fog, especially the area around San Francisco. At Point Reyes, just north of San Francisco Bay, a fog signal was installed as early as the 1870s, but it took numerous versions before one worked effectively in 1915. The dire need for such a signal was dramatically illustrated three years later, when Point Reyes reported their signal active for 2,139 hours.

Oregon's first lighthouse—slated to begin in 1851 on the Umpqua River (about midway up the state's coast) and finally started in 1857—was beset with numerous difficulties. One of several setbacks occurred due to a brawl between workers and residents. Building resumed, but six years after completion a storm claimed part of the lighthouse. The Lighthouse Board, afraid that

LEFT: **Named for the *Carrier Pigeon*, a clipper ship that was wrecked on the site in 1853, Pigeon Point Lighthouse towers above the fog-shrouded coast.** *Pescadero, California*

OPPOSITE: **Nestled high above the Pacific, the sixteen-sided Point Reyes Lighthouse overlooks the north entrance of San Francisco Bay. The dangerously rocky site required workers to fashion a flat expanse for construction.** *Point Reyes National Seashore, California*

A circuitous route
through the Siuslaw
National Forest snakes
its way to Heceta Head
Lighthouse. The pic-
turesque setting
makes it a popular
destination for visitors
to this rugged coast.
Florence, Oregon

Falling prey to
vandals after its use
was discontinued in
1939, Coquille River
Lighthouse was
acquired by the
state of Oregon and
the Army Corps of
Engineers in 1960;
its structure and
stucco finish were
later restored.
*Bullards Beach /
State Park, Oregon*

another storm would bring down the building, ordered the lens removed. In the midst of that task, the workers had to race down the stairs and out of the tower, which had begun shaking violently. Reaching safety below, they looked on helplessly as the building collapsed. Finally another station was completed in 1894; that one still stands.

Slightly north of the Umpqua is the Heceta Head Lighthouse in the spectacular setting of the Siuslaw National Forest. Lighted in 1894, the station still retains several of its original buildings. Perched on a promontory a little farther up the coast, in Newport, the Yaquina Head

Lighthouse was built on that spot when materials meant for a lighthouse at Cape Foulweather (four miles away) were inadvertently brought there. Landing supplies on the rocky slope was tricky, and several cargoloads were lost, including part of the lens.

Washington's island-strewn Puget Sound is a natural setting for lighthouses. The first was located on Whidbey Island, to guide vessels into the sound from the Strait of Juan de Fuca. Later moved to a nearby site, the Admiralty Head Lighthouse is now part of Fort Casey State Park. The West Point Lighthouse ushers ships heading through the sound to the port of Seattle.

Blanketed with trees and wrapped in mist, the craggy shores of central Oregon provide a splendid backdrop for the conical masonry tower of Heceta Head Lighthouse. *Florence, Oregon*

CANADA

The easternmost point of North America, Cape Spear, also houses the most easterly lighthouse on the continent, the first built in Newfoundland. Near St. John's, it is now surrounded by the 121 acres of Cape Spear National Historic Park. Newfoundland is also home to the Cape Bonavista Lighthouse, near the site where famed seventeenth-century explorer John Cabot is thought to have landed. Designed in England, the old building (now joined by a more modern incarnation) still holds the original lanterns that once glowed in the renowned Bell Rock Lighthouse in Scotland.

Because of the need to make lighthouses more visible by day, various regions developed distinctive uses of color on their lighthouses. Just as the southern United States display many variations on the black-and-white pattern, numerous lighthouses in Canada (and in northern Maine as well) feature vivid red accents to help set off the white towers from the bleak, snow-covered landscape. Towers following this distinctive color scheme include those at Prince Edward Island's Covehead (strewn with bright red details); Nova Scotia's Peggy's Cove (capped with red), Cape North (painted in a striking checkerboard pattern), and Seal Island and Halifax Harbour (both with wide horizontal bands alternating in red and white); and New Brunswick's Head Harbour (bold red stripes form a cross against the white). The usually snow-bound lighthouse at Rivière à las Martre on the St. Lawrence River is entirely red, except for a white stripe down the seaward side to provide contrast in summer and fall.

FOLLOWING PAGE:
Head Harbour Light, bearing distinctive markings similar to the Cross of St. George, keeps watch over the potentially threatening waters of the North Atlantic. *Campobello Island, New Brunswick, Canada*

LEFT: **Adorned in the red and white typical of many of the region's lighthouses, Peggy's Cove Lighthouse warns ships off the treacherously rocky coast. *Nova Scotia, Canada***

OPPOSITE: **Sheltered from the ravages of the Atlantic by Newfoundland and Nova Scotia, Prince Edward Island is spared some of the seafaring perils of neighboring eastern regions. But short-range lights, like Covehead Lighthouse on the northern coast, are essential for navigating the area. *Prince Edward Island National Park, Canada***

AFTERWORD

LOOKING TO THE FUTURE

Despite the modernization of lighthouses through automation, there is a growing debate over removing the human element in all situations. In Great Britain, where our North American lighthouse heritage originated, local groups have begun reestablishing lighthouse keepers in facilities that once had been automated. One such organization, the Sea Safety Group in Cornwall, was launched as a nonprofit organization to reinstate keepers in all forty-three local lighthouses.

"New technology will never replace the experienced human eye and intimate knowledge of local tides and coastline," Peter Raymond, a director of the Sea Safety Group, stated in the *Weekly Telegraph*. "While the new British coastguard centers are coordinating rescues thousands of miles away with the use of satellite-links," he explained, "we have tragedies not being detected in time that are happening just hundreds of yards off our coast."

As recently as December 1994, a similar debate was being held in western Canada, where the government was considering the destaffing of all thirty-five manned lightstations on the west coast, and planning to replace their keepers with automated weather observation systems.

Although lighthouses, with their simple yet immensely strong appearance, have long been seen as stalwarts of the American landscape, never-ending beacons to those who travel the waters, many today can rightfully be classified as endangered. Neglect, lack of funds for maintenance and repair, coastline erosion, and other factors all threaten to destroy many of these historic structures.

"Though they have long been regarded as immortal beacons, lighthouses cannot be taken for granted," noted James Hyland, president of the

OPPOSITE: **The compact, cylindrical iron tower of Nobska Point Lighthouse guards the junction of Nantucket Sound and Vineyard Sound from Woods Hole Harbor. *Cape Cod, Massachusetts***

Lighthouse Preservation Society, located in Rockport, Massachusetts. "Many have been abandoned and are falling into disrepair."

When Cape Cod Light was built in 1796, the Truro Bluffs on which it was erected stood 510 feet from the coastline of Massachusetts. Today, the elements have reduced that distance to just 125 feet and threaten still further erosion. More than forty feet of that distance was lost in a single winter storm in 1990. A similar fate is creeping up on nearby Nauset Lighthouse in Eastham, Massachusetts.

The Cape Hatteras Light in North Carolina also faces the onslaught of the Atlantic Ocean. Funding is being sought to rebuild the beach around it as a stopgap measure; this would allow time for funds to be raised to attempt to move the lighthouse to a safer location. The beach reconstruction alone, however, carries an estimated price of $3–4 million.

Nearly eight hundred lighthouses still remain; exactly how many of them are in imminent danger is unknown. The nonprofit Lighthouse Preservation Society is working at a national level to secure funding and policies to protect the structures, and localized groups have sprung up to protect individual lighthouses in many areas. A resurgent interest in lighthouses, complete with collectibles, conferences, tours, publications, and films, is also providing fuel for a much-needed conservationist movement.

At 193 feet, the Cape Hatteras Lighthouse is the tallest in the United States, and, due to the vagaries of the Gulf Stream, the guardian of the most dangerous stretch of the southern coast. *Buxton, Dare County, North Carolina*

A
CHRONOLOGY
OF
HISTORIC
LIGHTHOUSES

Its slender grace belying the strength and durability of its brick and steel construction, the Currituck Beach Lighthouse stands at the halfway point between the lights at Cape Henry and Bodie Island. *Corolla, North Carolina*

1716	Boston Light, with an 89-foot tower; the first lighthouse built in the United States
1767	Charleston Lighthouse, with a 161-foot tower, just off the southern tip of Morris Island, South Carolina
1771	Cape Ann Light on the east side of Thatcher Island, Massachusetts, with a 124-foot tower
1784	Great Point Lighthouse on the northern tip of Nantucket Island, Massachusetts, with a 71-foot tower
1788	Newburyport Harbor Light on Plum Island, Massachusetts
1791	Tybee Light, with a 145-foot tower, at the northern end of Tybee Island, Georgia; Cape Henry Lighthouse, with a 163-foot tower, on Cape Henry, Virginia, at the southern entrance to Chesapeake Bay
1795	Sequin Island Light on the island just south of the mouth of the Kennebec River, Maine, with a 53-foot tower
1797	Montauk Point Lighthouse on the east end of Long Island, New York, with a 108-foot tower
1798	Bakers Island Light on the north part of Bakers Island, Massachusetts; Cape Hatteras Lighthouse on the cape in North Carolina, with a 193-foot tower; Ocracoke Light, with a 76-foot tower, at the western end of Ocracoke Island, North Carolina
1799	Gay Head Lighthouse, with a 51-foot tower, on the west end of Martha's Vineyard Island, Massachusetts
1801	Georgetown Light, with an 87-foot tower, at the entrance to Winyah Bay, South Carolina
1808	Wood Island Lighthouse on the east end of the island in Maine, with a tower connected to the keeper's quarters; Chatham Light on the west side of Chatham Harbor, Massachusetts, with a 48-foot tower
1811	St. Simons Light, with a 106-foot tower, on the north side of the entrance to St. Simons Sound, Georgia; Boon Island Lighthouse at 133 feet above the water on this island 6.5 miles from mainland Maine
1812	Cape Lookout Light, with a 169-foot tower, at the northern tip of Cape Lookout, North Carolina
1816	Race Point Lighthouse on the northwestern tip of Cape Cod, Massachusetts, with a 66-foot tower
1821	Isles of Shoals Light, with a 58-foot tower, on White Island, New Hampshire
1822	Mobile Point Lighthouse, with a 59-foot girder tower, at Fort Morgan, Alabama
1823	Cape May Light, with a 170-foot tower, at Cape May, New Jersey
1824	St. Augustine Light, with a 161-foot tower, at the northern tip of Anastasia Island, Florida; Monhegan Island Lighthouse on Monhegan Island, Maine, with a 47-foot tower
1825	Key West Lighthouse, with an 86-foot tower, on Key West Island, Florida; Pensacola Light, with a 171-foot tower, on the north side of Chocatawhatchee Bay, Florida
1826	Dry Tortugas Lighthouse, with a 157-foot tower, on Loggerhead Key, Florida; Sand Key Light, with a girder tower, on the Sand Key, Florida
1827	Matinicus Rock Lighthouse, with a 48-foot tower, on the southern end of Matinicus Rock, Maine, at a point 90 feet above the water; Fire Island Light, with a 167-foot tower, on Fire Island, New York; Cape Charles Lighthouse, with a 191-foot tower, on Smith Island, Virginia
1829	Cape Elizabeth Lighthouse, with 67-foot tower, at the south entrance to Portland Harbor, Maine
1830	The 58-foot, granite tower of Mount Desert Lighthouse on Mount Desert Rock, Maine

1831   St. Marks Lighthouse, with an 80-foot tower, at the mouth of St. Marks River in Apalachee Bay, Florida; South Pass Light, with a girder tower, on South Pass, Louisiana; Whaleback Light at the entrance to Portsmouth Harbor, New Hampshire, with a 75-foot tower

1832   Eastern Point Light at the entrance to Gloucester Harbor, Massachusetts, with a 36-foot tower

1833   Cape St. George Light, with a 74-foot tower, on the western end of Cape St. George, Florida; Goat Island Lighthouse on the island at the entrance to Cape Porpoise Harbor, Maine, at 38 feet above the water; Assateague Light, with a 142-foot tower, on Assateague Island, Virginia

1835   Straitsmouth Light at the entrance to Rockport Harbor, Massachusetts

1836   Gun Cay Lighthouse on the southern tip of Gun Cay, Florida; Marblehead Light, with a 105-foot tower, at the northern tip of Marblehead Neck, Massachusetts

1838   Sand Island Light, with a 132-foot tower, on the west side of the entrance to Mobile Bay, Alabama

1839   Amelia Island Light, with a 64-foot tower, at the northern end of Amelia Island, Florida; Nauset Beach Lighthouse at Eastham, Massachusetts, with an 18-foot tower, later replaced with a 48-foot tower

1847   Little Machipongo Light, atop a watchtower, at the northern tip of Hog Island, Virginia

1848   Cape Canaveral Lighthouse, with a 145-foot tower, on Canaveral Cape, Florida; Egmont Key Light, with an 87-foot tower, on Egmont Key, Florida; Chandeleur Lighthouse, with a girder tower, on the northernmost point of Chandeleur Island, Louisiana; Bodie Island Light, with a 163-foot tower, on Bodie Island, North Carolina

1849   Cape San Las Lighthouse, with a girder tower, on Cape San Las, Florida

1850   Minots Ledge Lighthouse, with a 97-foot tower, at the south entrance to Boston Bay, Massachusetts; Sankaty Head Light, with a 70-foot tower, on the east end of Nantucket Island, Massachusetts

1852   Carysfort Reef Lighthouse on a line of reefs off the coast of Florida; Matagorda Lighthouse, with a 90-foot tower, at the Pass Cavallo entrance to Matagorda Bay, Texas

1853   Ship Island Light, with a 55-foot tower, at the west end of Ship Island, Mississippi

1855   Point Pinos Lighthouse, with a 43-foot tower, on the south side of Monterey Bay, California

1856   Crescent City Light, with a 45-foot tower, on Battery Point, California; Point Conception Lighthouse, with a 52-foot tower, on the north side of the Santa Barbara Channel, California; Santa Barbara Light, with a 24-foot tower, on the Santa Barbara Landing, California; Table Bluff Lighthouse, with a 35-foot tower, on Table Bluff, California; Cape Disappointment, with a 53-foot tower, at the mouth of the Columbia River, Washington

1857   Barataria Bay Light, with a 71-foot tower, on Fort Livingston, Louisiana; Umpqua River Lighthouse, with a 65-foot tower, at the mouth of the Umpqua River, Oregon; Cape Flattery Light, with a 65-foot tower, on Tatoosh Island, Washington

1858   Fenwick Island Lighthouse, with a 87-foot tower, on Fenwick Island, Delaware; Willapa Bay Light, with a 64-foot tower, on Cape Choalwater, Washington

1859   Great Isaac Light, with a 137-foot tower, on Great Isaac Island, Florida; Ship Shoal Lighthouse, with a girder tower, in the water off Ship Shoal, Louisiana

1860   Jupiter Inlet Light, with a 105-foot tower, on the north side of Jupiter Inlet, Florida

1866   Cape Arago Lighthouse, with a 44-foot tower, on Cape Arago, Oregon

1868   Cape Mendocino Lighthouse, with a 43-foot tower, on the west side of Cape Mendocino, California

1869   Santa Cruz Lighthouse, with a 39-foot tower, on the west side of Santa Cruz Harbor, California

1870   Point Arena Lighthouse, with a 115-foot tower, on Point Arena, California; Point Reyes Light, with a 37-foot tower, on the west end of Point Reyes, California; Cape Blanco Lighthouse, with a 59-foot tower, on the western end of Cape Blanco, Oregon

1871   Trinidad Head Light, with a 25-foot tower, on the head of Trinidad Head, California; the aptly named Halfway Rock Lighthouse's 77-foot tower, between Cape Elizabeth and Cape Small Point

1872   Pigeon Point Light, with a 115-foot tower, on Pigeon Point, California

1873   Alligator Reef Lighthouse, with a girder tower, on Alligator Reef, Florida; Yaquina Head Light, with a 93-foot tower, on Yaquina Head, Oregon

1874   Point Fermin Lighthouse, with a girder tower, on the point south of San Pedro, California; Point Hueneme Lighthouse, with a 48-foot tower, at the east entrance to Santa Barbara Channel, California; Horn Island Light, in the water off Petit Bois Island, Mississippi; Hereford Inlet Lighthouse, with a 55-foot tower, on the south side of Hereford Inlet, New Jersey

1875   Piedra Blancas Lighthouse, with a 74-foot tower, on Point San Luis, California; Point Montara Light, with a 30-foot tower, on Point Montara, California; Block Island Light, with a 67-foot tower, on Mohegan Bluffs at the east end of Block Island, Massachusetts; Currituck Beach Lighthouse, with a 163-foot tower, at Currituck Beach, North Carolina

1878   Fowey Rocks Light on a Florida reef, with a girder tower; South Pass West Jetty Lighthouse, with a 35-foot tower, at the ocean end of South Pass West Jetty, Louisiana

1880   American Shoal Light, with a girder tower, on American Shoal, Florida

1881   Tillamook Rock Light, with a 62-foot tower, on Tillamook Rock, Oregon

1884   Sanibel Island Lighthouse, with a 102-foot tower, on the north point of the Sanibel Island, Florida

Bathed in warm afternoon sun, the tower that now stands watch over the Edgartown breakwater is actually the old Essex Light from Ipswich, built in 1875 and reassembled at Edgartown in 1939. *Martha's Vineyard, Massachusetts*

Silhouetted by a glorious sunset, Grand Haven South Pierhead Inner Light is similar in design to other prominent lights on the eastern shore of Lake Michigan. *Grand Haven, Michigan*

1885	Point Loma Light, with a girder tower, on the west side of the entrance to San Diego Bay, California; Ludlam Beach Light, with a 35-foot tower, at Sea Isle City, New Jersey
1886	Rebecca Shoal Lighthouse, with a girder tower, in the water off Rebecca Shoal, Florida
1887	Anclote Keys Light, with a 102-foot tower, on the south point of Anclote Keys, Florida
1888	Ponce De Leon Lighthouse, with a 168-foot tower, north of the entrance to Ponce De Leon Inlet, Florida
1889	Point Sur Light, with a 50-foot tower, at the west end of Point Sur, California
1890	San Luis Obispo Light, with a 40-foot tower, on Point San Luis, California; Cape Meares Light, with a 38-foot tower, on the west end of Cape Meares, Oregon
1891	St. George Reef Light, with a 150-foot tower, on Seal Rock, California; Scituate North Jetty Lighthouse on a breakwater at the opening of Scituate Harbor, Massachusetts; Destruction Island Light, with a 94-foot tower, on Destruction Island, Washington
1894	Heceta Head Lighthouse, with a 56-foot tower, on Heceta Head, Oregon
1895	Crooked River Light, with a girder tower, near Carrabelle, Florida
1896	Sea Girt Lighthouse on the south side of Shark River Inlet, New Jersey; Brazos River Light, with a 103-foot tower, at the mouth of the Brazos River into Freeport Harbor, Texas
1898	Grays Harbor Lighthouse, with a 107-foot tower, on Point Chehalis, Washington; North Head Light, with a 65-foot tower, on the west side of Cape Disappointment, Washington
1901	Point Arguello Lighthouse, with a girder tower, on Point Arguello, California.
1902	St. Joseph Point Light, with a 41-foot tower, near Beacon Hill, Florida
1903	Scotch Cap Light, with a 50-foot tower, on Unimak Island, Alaska; Tree Point Lighthouse, with a 66-foot tower, on Tree Point, Alaska; Cape Fear Lighthouse, with a 161-foot tower, on Smith Island, North Carolina
1905	The Graves Light on the southeastern side of the South Channel entrance to Boston Harbor, Massachusetts
1906	Kawaihae Light, with a 36-foot tower, at Kawaihae Bay, Hawaii; Keahole Point Lighthouse, with a 33-foot tower, on Keahole Point, Hawaii
1907	Hillsboro Inlet Lighthouse, with a 137-foot tower, on the north side of the inlet in Florida; Pepeekeo Point Light, with a girder tower, and Paukaa Point Light, with a girder tower, at Hilo Bay, Hawaii
1908	Napoopoo Lighthouse, with a 22-foot tower, on Cook Point, Hawaii; Sabine Pass East Jetty Light, with a girder tower, on the end of Sabine Pass East Jetty, Texas
1909	Point Cabrillo Light, with a girder tower, on Point Cabrillo, California
1910	Cape Hinchinbrook Lighthouse, with a 67-foot tower, at the entrance to Prince William Sound, Alaska
1911	Kukuihaele Light, with a 34-foot tower, on Kukuihaele Island, Hawaii
1912	Anacapa Island Lighthouse, with a girder tower, on the east end Anacapa Island, California; Kauhola Point Light, with an 85-foot tower, on the northern side of Kauhola Island, Hawaii
1913	Cape Spencer Lighthouse, with a 25-foot tower, on Cape Spencer, Alaska; Los Angeles Light, with a 69-foot tower, on the San Pedro Breakwater near Los Angeles, California
1915	Cedar Keys North Bank Light, with a girder tower, in the water at the Northwest Channel entrance to Cedar Keys, Florida
1916	Cape St. Elias Light, with a 55-foot tower, on Kayak Island, Alaska; Galveston Jetty Lighthouse, with a 90-foot tower, on Galveston Jetty, Texas
1921	Pacific Reef Light, with a girder tower, in the water on Pacific Reef, Florida; Molasses Reef Lighthouse, with a girder tower, in the water on Molasses Reef, Florida
1922	Seahorse Reef Lighthouse, with a girder tower, in the water at the south end of Seahorse Reef, Florida
1926	Point Vicente Light, with a 67-foot tower, on Point Vicente, California
1927	Riding Rock Lighthouse, with a girder tower, on Castle Rock, Florida
1929	Cape Decision Light, with a 75-foot tower, on Cape Decision, Alaska; Cape Kumukahi Lighthouse, with a girder tower, on Cape Kumukahi, Hawaii
1931	Shinnecock Light on the west side of Shinnecock Inlet, New York
1933	Smith Shoal Light, with a girder tower, in the water off Smith Shoal, Florida; Tennessee Reef Lighthouse, with a girder tower, on Tennessee Reef, Florida
1935	Pulaski Shoal Light, with a girder tower, in the water off Pulaski Shoal, Florida; Cosgrove Shoal Lighthouse, with a girder tower, in the water off Cosgrove Shoal, Florida
1938	Atlantic City Lighthouse, with a girder tower, on the south side of Absecon Inlet, New Jersey
1939	North Rock Light, with a girder tower, at the northern end of North Bimini Island, Florida

OPPOSITE: With its compact Gothic tower, Lime Kiln Point Lighthouse glows in the sunlight over Puget Sound. *San Juan Island, Washington*

INDEX